a
time to
speak

COMPILED BY
HENRIETTA GAMBILL

Cincinnati, Ohio

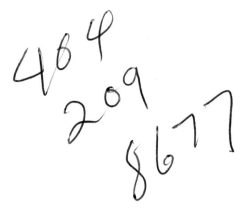

Library of Congress Cataloging-in-Publication Data

A time to speak / compiled by Henrietta Gambill.
       p.   cm.
   Includes index.
   ISBN 0-7847-0786-3 (pbk.)
    1. Holidays—United States—Religious aspects—Meditations.
  2. Special days—United States—Religious aspects—Meditations.
GT4803.A2T55 1998
242'.2—dc21   97-30447

                                 CIP

The Standard Publishing Company, Cincinnati, Ohio
A division of Standex International Corporation
© 1998 by The Standard Publishing Company
All rights reserved
Printed in the United States of America
05 04 03 02 01 00 99 98   5 4 3 2 1

Introduction

Special days call for special words. On holidays and special occasions, we pause, think, remember, and "take stock." Christians asked to speak publicly at these times—in worship, to a Sunday school class, to the PTA or other civic organizations—have a unique opportunity to influence their listeners toward God.

A *Time to Speak* provides fifty-two short meditations on seventeen different special days and times throughout the year. Meditations for all major holidays, plus other occasions such as graduation and even tax time, are included. Each talk touches on the history, the significance, and the Christian perspective of the special times in our lives.

For anyone called on to speak formally or simply to an informal gathering of neighbors, *A Time to Speak* provides just the right thoughts for any special occasion.

CONTENTS

New Year's Day

RESOLUTIONS

1 John 4:4

As you tear off that last leaf of your day-by-day calendar, think of it this way: "I'm starting clean, with a new leaf. Or, to be more exact, 365 new leaves (one more, of course, if it's leap year).

It's a good time to look backward—to finally analyze the soon-to-be-ending past 365 days, and planning the next 365 (or 366). Think back. Just what resolutions did you make when you entered this year? Be honest now: how many are actually unbroken? How long did most of them last? Which one did you totally forget about, or ignore?

Resolutions have no value whatsoever if they are ignored. Their essential purposes and objectives are worthless unless adhered to consistently. Benjamin Franklin was aware of some personal habits that he considered counter-productive to good living, and he drew up a set of resolutions to guide him in conquering those habits. He had only the best of intentions. To his chagrin, however, he found himself in violation of one after another until he was obliged to admit he had not progressed at all!

We who are Christ's have available precise and proper power to make and keep each resolution. This power is the indwelling Holy Spirit!

Brant Lee Doty

When you were buried to sin in your baptism, you began a new life with the Spirit of God as a resident of your heart, a guide for your life.

Listen to Him! He will guide you in distinguishing good and evil. When He speaks—silently, but clearly through your educated conscience—listen!

Then follow His guidance.

New Year's Day

GIFT, OPPORTUNITY, RESPONSIBILITY

Psalm 90:12, KJV; Matthew 25:14-30;
Acts 17:28; Ephesians 5:16, KJV

The beginning of another year reminds us that the Lord God is sovereign in His universe. He determines the boundaries and limitations of time. "In him we live and move and have our being" (Acts 17:28).

Time is a precious commodity to be used well in the new year. To do this we must come to understand that time is a gift.

A widower whose wife had died at a relatively young age said, "If we had known we had so little time left to be together, we would have lived our lives much differently than we did. I thought we had a lot of time left to do this or do that." When we recognize that time is in the hands of God, that it is a gift from God, we become much more appreciative of time.

Time is not only a gift, time is also an opportunity. In the parable of the talents (Matthew 25:14-30), Jesus speaks of the master giving certain responsibilities to his servants and then going away for a long time. The opportunity lay in the gap between the time the master left and the moment he returned. Each person with a gift had opportunity to invest it well and use it

E. Ray Jones

wisely. Two invested wisely and one did not. Therein lay their eternal destiny.

Today may be our only opportunity to both speak kind words and do kind deeds. Today we have the opportunity to make decisions that set the direction of our lives.

Time is not only a gift and an opportunity, the use of time is a responsibility. Paul tells us to redeem the time (Ephesians 5:16, KJV). We must make the most of it. Use it wisely. We have the responsibility to use time to develop ourselves as persons. We have the responsibility to use time to reach others and bring them to Christ.

We don't know when the management of time will be removed from our care and eternity will be ushered in. Since that is true, we need to take the gift of time, see it as an opportunity, and act responsibly with it.

"So teach us to number our days, that we may apply our hearts unto wisdom" (Psalm 90:12, KJV).

NEW YEAR'S DAY

NEW BEGINNINGS

Proverbs 3:6; Zechariah 4:6; James 4:2

Perhaps we get our love of new beginnings from God. After all, His mercies are new every morning. He's the God of second chances, of fresh starts, of new songs. There is no greater second chance than salvation, when we are born again!

And no day of the entire year symbolizes starting afresh more than New Year's Day. Many of us weigh this day down with our good intentions—this is the day we finally intend to get serious about diets and time management and exercise programs and studying the Bible and giving up all our bad habits and taking on good habits. We all long to be successful and have victorious, meaningful, worthy lives. We remind ourselves that one of the fruit of the Spirit listed in Galatians is self-control.

But most of the time, no matter how desperate we are to change and reach our goals, our New Year's resolutions derail year after year. In disappointment and disgust, after a few days or a few weeks, we give up on ourselves for the rest of the year. Maybe we even join the ranks of people who joke about this day, vowing from now on the only thing they'll ever give up again is making New Year's resolutions.

How easy it is to forget that the battle is not ours, but the Lord's. "'Not by might nor by

Maria Anne Tolar

power, but by my Spirit,' says the Lord almighty" (Zechariah 4:6). In Proverbs 3:6 we are told, "In all your ways acknowledge him, and he will make your paths straight."

We should honor the resolutions we make this day by taking them to God in prayer and asking His help, His wisdom. James 4:2 reminds us that we have not because we ask not. Because God is good and His grace is sufficient, because He is for us and not against us, because we can do all things through Christ who strengthens us, we have 365 blessed days to pray our way to victory this year.

NEW YEAR'S DAY

NEW YEAR'S DAY

Philippians 3:13, 14

January, the first month of the modern calendar, received its name from Janus, one of the gods worshiped by the ancient Romans. Janus was often depicted with two faces, one peering to the past and the other to the future. He was also sometimes shown with a staff in one hand and keys in the other, signifying his work as a closer and an opener. Even though we reject the religious significance that the Romans attached to Janus, that significance does seem appropriate to us as we contemplate the beginning of a New Year.

First of all, New Year's Day gives us an opportunity to pause and look back over what we have experienced during the past twelve months. Some of these experiences may be happy ones—new friends gained, growth in our church, or other victories for the Lord's kingdom. But some of them may be sad—the death of a friend or family member, the loss of a job, or even more painful, our succumbing to Satan's wiles and falling into some grievous sin.

January is a closer but it is also an opener. As we stand at the beginning of this new year, we need to recognize that it offers unnumbered opportunities for wonderful victories—situations that will allow us to grow spiritually and

John W. Wade

ways to develop new skills and make new friends that can lead to the glory of Christ and His kingdom.

Once when Winston Churchill was asked what the best year of his life was, he replied, "Next year." Christians ought to take the same optimistic view of the new year, that the new year holds all the potential for being the greatest year of our lives.

In writing to the Philippians, Paul expressed a similar idea: "Forgetting what is behind and straining toward what is ahead, I press on toward the goal to win the prize for which God has called me heavenward in Christ Jesus" (3:13, 14). As we begin this new year, may we forget the things in the past that may hamper us in the future. Then let us press on to the goal that our Lord has set before us.

VALENTINE'S DAY

THE HEART-SHAPED HOLIDAY

1 John 4:9, 10

"Be my Valentine!" implore countless heart-shaped and heart-decorated red greeting cards each February. February 14 brings smiles to sweethearts, family members, and friends as they receive mementos of affection on this the most romantic of our holidays.

The history of Valentine's Day is not easy to unravel. Roman history tells us of two Saint Valentines who, during the third century, were beheaded for their faith on February 14. One was a priest in Rome and the other was the bishop in a town about sixty miles from Rome. There is debate as to whether they were two people or whether one person was associated with both places.

Be that as it may, the associations of February 14 today seem far from its third century beginnings. Some authorities link Valentine's Day to a Roman festival, the *Lupercalia,* which began on February 15 and included, the night before, the pairing of boys and girls to be partners during the festival. Other stories link the day to Saint Valentine himself. According to one such story, the Emperor Claudius II, on the assumption that single men make the best soldiers, forbade marriage. Valentine, however, defied the order and performed marriages.

Ward Patterson

a
time to
speak

The oldest hand-made valentines in America are nearly three hundred years old. Commercial valentines made their appearance about two hundred years ago. Designs and styles have come and gone, but today valentines are very big business indeed. Towns like Darling, Pennsylvania, and Romance, Arkansas, have post offices that do a thriving business remailing thousands of valentines each year.

"Be my Valentine!" The day appeals to our deepest emotions. Its popularity reminds us that there is a basic human need to love and be loved. The Bible's central message is that God loves us and that He sent a message and a Messenger to make His love known. John wrote, "This is how God showed his love among us: He sent his one and only Son into the world that we might live through him. This is love: not that we loved God, but that he loved us and sent his Son as an atoning sacrifice for our sins" (1 John 4:9, 10). Now that's a heart-shaped valentine!

VALENTINE'S DAY

VALENTINE'S DAY

John 3:16

It used to be the custom in elementary school classes that you bought a valentine for everyone in the class. Money was scarce so you bought a packet of cheap ones. Then came the job of deciding which one would go to which class-mate. There were the not even faintly romantic ones you addressed to your friends. There were the slightly romantic ones you directed to those you really liked. There were the non-committal ones reserved for those to whom (given a choice) you'd have sent no valentine at all. But the teacher said you should have one for each member of the class.

We always counted the valentines we got to see if we got as many as we gave. We read care-fully each one looking for the hidden meaning, wondering who counted us as friend, who counted us as more than friend, and who would not have counted us at all unless it was required.

When we grow up we find that most people fall into those same three categories of friends, family and those to whom we are indifferent. There is the love of friendship. The Bible has a word for that kind of love; the word from which Philadelphia gets its name.

Then there are those whom we love in the romantic sense. The Bible has no word for that,

Robert C. Shannon

but we do. That word becomes the foundation for those whom we love in the sense of family. The Bible does have a word for that.

Then there are those who are neither friend nor family. You couldn't like them even if you tried. Yet, as Christians, we cannot be indifferent to them. We can only love them with that special love that Jesus had for us. It's interesting that the only Greek word that all regular church attenders know is the word for this kind of love: *agape.* With this kind of love, God loves us all.

"God so loved the world." What a big heart God has! Like that class in school so long ago, no one is left out. It's a big leap to take today from the sentimental love of Valentine's Day to the supernatural love God has for us and we have for others. But we can do it.

VALENTINE'S DAY

"I LOVE YOU"

Luke 10:27

Valentine's Day has become big business. Christmas is barely past when stores begin displaying the big red and pink lacy hearts. It's a day set aside to tell the special people in your life that you love them. You can't miss it. You don't dare forget it!

The card and flower shops abound with suggestions for showing special people we love them. Restaurants offer special meals. Cupid with his bow and arrow seems to be everywhere! Secret admirers come out of hiding in hopes of being noticed by the objects of their affections.

Hearts and flowers, a fancy box of chocolate candy, fat little cherubs with bows and arrows. It's funny what we choose to symbolize our love!

Valentine's Day is a day set aside to celebrate love. And far too often, the celebration ends when Valentine's Day ends. It's easy to say "I love you" when everyone else is saying it, too. But what about saying "I love you" when it's not so easy? What about saying "I love you" to someone who's not so lovable, or someone who doesn't feel worthy of being loved?

One day out of the year is not enough to say "I love you." Those we love shouldn't have to

*Patricia M.
Sorensen*

wait until Valentine's Day to know that we love them. We should say it (and show it) often enough that they don't doubt it. They should know that we love them unconditionally, like Jesus loves us, every day of the year.

What symbols would you choose to show your love—hearts, flowers, cupids? God chose different symbols to show His love for us—a cross, a crown of thorns, and an empty tomb.

Do you really want to show someone that you love him today? Tell him about Jesus. Tell him that Jesus loves him. That's a celebration of love that will last for eternity.

Valentine's Day

The Gift of Love

1 Corinthians 13:1

Valentine's Day is celebrated each year on February 14th by exchanging romantic and even comic messages. We call these messages valentines and we send them to the special people in our lives.

Love is universal. It affects all classes, all groups of people. Does one need a significant other to be able to celebrate Valentine's Day? No, it's a day of love and of the heart.

On a television show, a person was asked what she would desire if she could have one wish. Would she ask for a million dollars, good health, a bigger house, a better job? This young person looked thoughtful for a moment. Her answer surprised me. She said that her greatest wish was to be loved.

She is right—the greatest gift for any heart is to be loved. All the money in the world, the health, the power, anything you can think of, cannot surpass being loved.

The person who loves you may not be perfect but that doesn't matter. Human love is imperfect. If your husband doesn't send you flowers or buy you candy, it doesn't mean that he doesn't love you. If that special person at school didn't put a terrific valentine in your box, it doesn't mean she's not thinking of you.

Kathleen A. Thompson

We do, or don't do, things for many reasons because our love is imperfect.

We have a wonderful God to lean on. His love is perfect. It isn't affected by moodiness, the weather, or by daily problems. He had only one Son, Jesus Christ, yet He was able to give Him to the world as a sacrifice for our sins. This is perfect love.

If you don't have someone to share Valentine's Day with, look around for someone who loves you and be grateful for him. Show your gratitude with a card, candy or a hug. Strive toward that perfect love, because love is the most important thing.

Give someone the greatest gift of all today— the gift of knowing someone loves him.

PRESIDENTS' DAY

HONOR THE OFFICE

Matthew 22:17-21; Acts 5:29; Romans 13:1, 7; 1 Peter 2:17

"Show proper respect to everyone . . . honor the king" (1 Peter 2:17).

The apostle Peter never wrote anything more surprising than that. Who was the king? Caesar! And he did not deserve the honor of anyone and certainly did not deserve the honor of Christians. The king was a pagan who thought himself divine. Persecution was already threatening the lives of believers, and persecution would be ordered by the king!

Surely the apostle meant that we should honor the office, not necessarily the one who occupies that office. So, in every age we can honor the office of governmental authority even when we cannot honor the person who holds that office.

If all presidents were like George Washington or Abraham Lincoln, it would be easy to honor the president. The fact is that there have been honorable men in that office and dishonorable men in that office. But we can honor the office even if we cannot honor the occupant of that office.

We can honor authority even when we disagree with the way that authority is being used. We can honor laws even if they are laws of

Robert C. Shannon

which we do not approve. As Christians we are to disobey the law only when obeying man's law would make us disobey God's law. Then we have to say with the apostle, "We must obey God rather then men!" (Acts 5:29).

As citizens of a free land, we can work to change our laws, and we should. But until the law is changed, it is the law. Jesus taught us to pay taxes (Matthew 22:17-21). Certainly taxes were then used for things of which Jesus did not approve. Today our taxes may be used for things of which we do not approve. But, like Jesus, we pay our taxes.

When the apostle Paul wrote a "tribute" in Romans 13:7, the meaning was taxes. The apostle Paul also taught us to be submissive to governmental authority (Romans 13:1).

The apostle Peter teaches us to honor those in authority. One thing we all can do, and must do. We must pray for our leaders, pray for our government, and pray for our country.

GOOD
FRIDAY

FREEDOM TO CHOOSE

Genesis 1:31; Romans 5:19

One year after the tragic crash of ValuJet flight 592, investigator John Gaglia remarked, "You can't regulate morality. We rely on the moral character of everybody in the system to comply with the regulations. We find that the majority of the people involved in this case did not comply."

God could have regulated morality. In fact, He could have insured morality and forced us to comply by creating us without a free will. But, in His wisdom and by His design, God gave every human being the right to make his own decisions, right or wrong. God saw what He had done and knew it was "very good" (Genesis 1:31).

Sadly, we took the freedom God gave us and brought something "very bad" into His "very good" world. That something was sin and all of its consequences. When Jesus came to die for our sins, He did not attempt to take away our freedom to choose. Instead, He came to clean up the mess we created when we made the wrong choices. His sacrifice on Calvary turned something "very bad" back into something "very good." Christ cleansed our hearts and restored our broken relationship with God.

Larry Jones

No, God does not regulate morality or force us to comply. He does, however, recreate us through the sacrifice of His Son. "For just as through the disobedience of the one man the many were made sinners, so also through the obedience of the one man the many will be made righteous" (Romans 5 :19). Since we have been rescued from our sins, we have a desire to do what is right as a means of pleasing the one who saved us.

Praise God! Life is good again because Christ Jesus made it good with His own blood.

GOOD FRIDAY

GOOD FRIDAY

Ephesians 3:20

The expression "Good Friday" refers to the day on which Jesus the Messiah, our Passover lamb, was sacrificed for us.

Let us think for a few moments about why this particular Friday is "good."

First, in the Jewish calendar, Nisan 14 fell on this day. It was the day when the Passover lambs were sacrificed in the temple during the afternoon. It was the day of preparation for the Passover feast that was observed in the evening of the same day. The Passover was the highest and most important of all the festivals on the Jewish calendar. It was a festival of remembrance, to bring before the minds of the people the fact that God redeemed them from Egypt with signs and wonders and an outstretched hand. It was the greatest good in the history of Israel.

Second, the highest good in the history of mankind was accomplished on this day. God is the one "who is able to do immeasurably more than all we ask or imagine" (Ephesians 3:20). He is the one who can turn tragedy into triumph. Think of the greatest failure, the most heinous sin of your life. Now think of God. He is the one who can take that sin and turn it into something good. We know this because the

Lonnie C. Mings

worst crime in the annals of mankind—the crucifixion of God's Son—was turned into the greatest good; that is, the salvation of the world. For this reason, that awful day—when the heavens turned black, the earth shook, and all nature mourned the death of its creator—that day has gone down in history as "Good" Friday.

Third, on this Friday, God acted in a way He had never done before. Allowing His Son to be nailed to a cross, He brought about the redemption of mankind. On this day God led captivity captive, slew death, and turned tragedy into triumph. Never before in a single day was so much good accomplished.

No wonder the day of His passion is called Good Friday.

GOOD FRIDAY

THE WEIGHT OF THE CROSS

Luke 23:34; 1 John 1:7

A visitor to a passion play once asked to see the cross that was used in the performance. Surprised at the weight, he exclaimed that he thought it would be hollow or made of a lighter wood. The actor portraying Jesus in the play said, "I must feel the weight of the cross to effectively act like Christ."

Many movies and plays have been produced about the life, death, and resurrection of Christ. We have been intrigued about His life, anguished at His crucifixion, and rejoiced at His resurrection. Somehow, though, the trek to Calvary may not have the impact it ought to. We remember Simon of Cyrene who was commanded to take the cross from Jesus. But think for a moment about what Jesus did. He had been stripped of His clothing, beaten severely, and a crown of thorns had been jammed into His skull. But then . . .

But then, He had to carry the very thing that would be an instrument in His death. It was like a criminal, sentenced to death, having to carry the gun for the firing squad or the rope for the hangman or the wires for the electric chair. It was one more act of cruelty for Jesus. It was, perhaps, a mockery from those who wanted Him shamed for all that He had done.

Don A. Stowell

Jesus went to His death willingly in order to fulfill God's plan to save His people. The words that were spoken from the cross, "Father, forgive them" (Luke 23:34), encourage us and give us hope. But it was the blood he shed from His head, His hands, His feet, and His side that "purifies us from all sin" (1 John 1:7).

Jesus bore the weight of the cross on the day we call "Good Friday" so that we might "walk in the light as he is in the light" (1 John 1:7).

GOOD
FRIDAY

JESUS' CRUCIFIXION

John 3:16

A missionary once made contact with an
African tribe that had never heard the gospel
message. After some discussion with the tribal
chief, he was allowed to speak to the tribal
leaders about Christ. He told of Jesus' birth and
how He ministered to the people, healing their
illnesses and even raising some from the dead.
The men listened intently and with obvious
delight as the life of Jesus was laid out before.
But when the missionary told the story of Jesus'
arrest, trial, and crucifixion, the mood of the
men changed dramatically. The old chief rose to
his feet and hurled his spear into the ground.
"If I had been there," he shouted, "I would
never have let them kill such a good man!"

It took the missionary several minutes before
he could calm the leaders down and try to
explain to them why it was necessary for Jesus
to die on the cross. But they were unwilling to
accept his explanation, and he had to spend
many months of further teaching before they
began to understand the meaning of Christ's
suffering and death.

We may pride ourselves on being more
sophisticated than these primitive tribal people.
Certainly we would never react so violently on
hearing the account of Jesus' crucifixion. But is

John W. Wade

it possible that our theological sophistication is really a mask for a rational acceptance of the crucifixion without ever involving our hearts in a commitment to its fuller meaning? Let us use this Good Friday as an opportunity to visualize Jesus' death for us in a deeper, fuller way that will cause us once again to kneel at the foot of the cross. Some use physical symbols such as a crucifix to emphasize the importance of Christ's death. Others object to the use of symbols fearing that such use may lead to attitudes that seem almost like idolatry.

When we contemplate the death of Christ, it might become more real and personal to us if we read John 3:16 in this fashion: "God so love me, that he gave his only begotten Son, that I should not perish, but have everlasting life" (KJV). We can then rise to face the world with the firm conviction that He really died for our sins.

Easter

What Does Easter Mean?

1 Corinthians 15:12-23

It's Easter! It's resurrection day! But what does that mean? It means that nearly two thousand years ago, Christ arose from the dead. But what does that mean to us today?

It means that there is a resurrection of the dead. There is hope even for this body of mine that has been humiliated by the presence of indwelling sin and death and decay. It will be changed to be like His glorious body.

It means that there is purpose in preaching the gospel and in believing it! Our Savior has proved that He is more than just a man; He is God the Son.

It means that the Word of God is found to be true for it lives and works in power, deep within our beings!

It means that Jesus Christ is alive! How do we know that is true? God's Word tells us. We can talk to Him and walk with Him. We cannot doubt that which we have actually experienced.

It means that our sins are gone, leaving us forgiven—at peace with God, and cleansed—at peace within because we no longer feel the weight of guilt.

It means believing that our dear ones, who have gone on before us, have not perished. They are not dead but are already living in

Elva Minette Martin

eternity! They are in the very presence of the risen, living Son of God.

If in this life only we had a hope in Christ, a hope of a resurrection that is only an unlikely possibility, we would be of all men most miserable.

"But Christ has indeed been raised from the dead, the firstfruits of those who have fallen asleep. For since death came through a man, the resurrection of the dead comes also through a man. For as in Adam all die, so in Christ all will be made alive" (1 Corinthians 15:12-23).

That is what Easter means!

EASTER

EASTER

1 Corinthians 15:20

In the Eastern Church, the most joyful festival of the year is Easter. The same church puts a heavy emphasis on matter, on the physical aspects of man and nature. They remind us that the Savior came not just to redeem spirits or souls, but also to redeem matter—in fact, to redeem the whole of creation. Judaism also emphasizes the physical aspects of life—the physical body, family life, joyful eating and drinking, the love of God's creation—in short, the physical world.

In the West an overspiritualized view of salvation has developed in which there is really very little need of a resurrected body. Salvation seems to consist of "souls" or disembodied spirits going to Heaven to enjoy a kind of nebulous existence.

It is good for us to remember that man is body as well as spirit. God fashioned the body from the dust of the ground and breathed into it the "breath of life"—that is, the spirit. Man will always be composed of two basic parts: body and spirit. A spirit without a body is naked, unclothed. A disembodied spirit is not complete; it is, in fact, in a slightly embarrassing condition.

Lonnie C. Mings

We need bodies. This is why Easter is so important.

The joy of the resurrection is that Christ conquered death and made it possible for us to have new bodies. He himself rose as the firstfruits of those who sleep, as we read in 1 Corinthians 15:20, "Christ has indeed been raised from the dead, the firstfruits of those who have fallen asleep."

"Firstfruits" implies that a general harvest will follow. So it will, and we shall participate in it if we have come to know Him through faith.

This is the joy of Easter.

EASTER

HE IS RISEN!

Matthew 28:5, 6

Spring comes with a burst of energy and new life. Crocuses thrust through packed soil, and trees throb with an inner life until their buds explode in technicolor bloom. All nature demands expression. But the resurrection of Jesus was not about springtime; there was nothing natural about it. It defied nature.

Consider the facts: Christ was crucified on the cross. His body was placed in the tomb. It disappeared. His friends and followers expected His death to be permanent and seemed resigned to the fact. Grief and terror crumpled their faith. However, when they entered the tomb, an angel declared, "He is risen!"

The resurrection of Jesus separates Christianity from all other religions. It certainly validated His life and death. As a historical fact, His resurrection can be accepted by anyone, but the power of His resurrection can be accepted and appropriated only by those who are responsive. Jesus' friends needed personal encounters with the risen Christ to ignite their faith. First, there was Mary Magdalene who didn't recognize Christ until He spoke to her. Then He walked and talked with the two on their way home to Emmaus. When they finally realized He was the risen Christ, they exclaimed,

Dorothy N. Snyder

"Did not our hearts burn within us?" And they couldn't wait to tell others. He appeared to His eleven apostles in the upper room and dissolved their doubts and gave them His peace. Later, He played host for a fish breakfast on the seashore and challenged His disciples to share His message.

To each of Christ's encounters with His disciples, He brought forgiveness, issued a challenge, and gave courage. His work was done; their work—taking the message of Jesus to everyone—was just beginning. His message persisted until a pagan world was conquered by a handful of enlightened followers.

There's a legend that when Satan was asked what he missed most in Heaven, he replied, "The sound of the trumpets in the morning."

Heaven seems nearer, doesn't it, when we can hear the trumpets join the chorus "He is risen!"

EASTER

THE BEST JOKE

Romans 16:19, 20

In the tradition of the ancient Russian Orthodox church, the day after Easter was devoted to telling jokes. Priests would join with people in unveiling their best jokes for one another. It was an interesting tradition of imitating the cosmic joke that God pulled on Satan in the Resurrection. Satan thought he won on Friday, but God had the last laugh on Sunday.

It is not our tradition to sit around and tell jokes for the same reasons, yet laughter is part of the joy we experience in our Christian lives. The realities that we face each day do not always make us happy. But if we are in Christ, we learn to deal with them. Because of Christ, we have inner joy in the face of trials.

Jesus died on the cross for us so that He might save us from sin. God raised Him up to conquer death and the grave so that we might live eternally with Him. God's plan did not end at the cross, because there would be little hope ahead for us. Instead, God chose to become victorious for us. That's what brings us joy!

Do you know what victory is? Victory is overcoming any obstacle that would keep you from doing what you need to do. For Jesus, it was overcoming death. For us, it could be winning a race, becoming debt free, or getting that job we

Don A. Stowell

always wanted. The ultimate victory for us is dying to sin and being risen with Christ. Then we are forgiven of our sins! Does that idea bring you joy? You may not realize this now, but when a person becomes a Christian, Satan is defeated again.

The Sunday that many call Easter is resurrection Sunday. Christians recognize it as a celebration of the risen Christ. He arose from darkness to reign forever. The victory is over Satan. As you rejoice today, keep in mind the message that the apostle Paul wrote to the Roman Christians: "I want you to be wise about what is good, and innocent about what is evil. The God of peace will soon crush Satan under your feet" (Romans 16:19, 20).

What victory!

Tax Time

OUR SLAVERY

Matthew 22:15-21

What we do at tax time is illegal, but what else can we do? We're working as slaves, and the law does not allow that. Against our will we're driven to toil without pay at a task we hate. The task of filling out our income tax return.

We feel like hating somebody or something. Shall we hate our country, or only the IRS? Maybe we should hate our congressman. At least we can vote against him. But what good should that do? The new congressman would vote for taxes too.

We can't live without taxes. That makes it hard to hate anyone involved in taxation. He's as helpless as we are. If we weren't taxed for law enforcement, we would have to buy a gun and sit up all night to keep thieves from stealing the doghouse in our backyard—and then probably they would shoot us and take the doghouse anyway. If we weren't taxed for schools, we'd have to spend half our time teaching our kids to read and write, add and subtract. If we weren't taxed for streets, how would we get to work, or to the store for groceries, or to the park for a picnic? No, cancel that last item. Without taxes there wouldn't be any park. If

Orrin Root

you think a minute, you can name some other good things that can't exist without taxes.

First-century people didn't like taxes any more than we do. That's why some troublemakers thought they could get Jesus in trouble by involving Him in the politics of taxation. "Is it right to pay taxes to Caesar?" they asked.

"Let's see the money you pay taxes with," Jesus responded. The coin was stamped with the head of Caesar. "So give Caesar what belongs to him," said Jesus (Matthew 22:15-21).

That head of Caesar on the coin was clear evidence that Caesar's government actually was in charge. It was providing good roads, law enforcement, and national defense. The taxpayers were benefiting from those; it was only fair to help pay for them.

Today we have our taxes still, because we still can't live without them. Hating doesn't seem to help. So what can we do about our slavery? Maybe we'd better just learn to love it.

TAX
TIME

TAX TIME

Matthew 16:24

Nobody gets pleasure from paying taxes. We have an old saying to the effect that there are only two certainties in life and they are death and taxes. (Actually, there are more certainties that these.) But, try as we may, we can't avoid paying taxes. April 15 isn't exactly the happiest day of the year for many Americans. We often lament, "It wouldn't be so bad if the government didn't waste so much of our hard-earned tax money on useless things."

But there is another way to look at taxes. They are essential if we are to keep our freedom. Our armed forces, which protect the freedoms we love, are kept at the highest level of effectiveness in the world through technology that is very expensive. Failure to maintain our effectiveness in this area can be terribly costly for all of us. Taxes sustain our freedoms. Taxes are needed if we are to maintain the transportation system on which our whole way of life depends. And the education of our children is made possible by the taxes we pay.

Law and order would evaporate if the tax base they rest on disappeared. Public health depends on many who inspect our food, medicines, water, and the air we breathe. Another old saying comes to mind: "There is no free

Henry E. Webb

lunch." The many things we have come to expect simply have to be paid for with money; they are not free.

There is another very costly matter that we share and that is our salvation. It is often said: "Salvation is free." That may be true for you and me, but it certainly wasn't true for God; it cost Him His Son. And it wasn't free for Jesus, either. What we have sometimes taken for granted, cost Jesus His life on the cross. We are saved by God's grace, but we must never think that God's grace, though freely extended, is cheap. It was not only costly for God; it has a price for every person who hears Jesus say, "If anyone would come after me, he must deny himself and take up his cross and follow me" (Matthew 16:24).

We are forever in debt to God for His great love!

MOTHER'S DAY

MOTHERS ARE SPECIAL

Ephesians 6:2

Mothers! Certainly one of God's greatest inventions! We all have them; they are indispensable!

They come in various sizes, shapes, and colors. Their hair may be red, yellow, brown, black, or, most gloriously, silvery gray and sparkling white. Body shapes vary to extremities of height, weight, and, within reasonable limits, contour.

All mothers have one thing in common, of course: God has created them with extra-special care to enable them to perpetuate the human race! And to God, through them, we give the glory.

It is more than likely that many of life's most vital lessons have been impressed on all of us through a mother's unselfish and unceasing attendance to our vital needs: food, shelter, and clothing, as well as her succinct ability to rebuke, commend, or instruct, according to the need or occasion. It is also likely that we have picked up numerous practical hints on good living, sometimes by the imposition of bodily discipline—richly deserved, of course! And through her we unconsciously learned the meaning and depths of unselfish love.

Brant Lee Doty

We are not alone when we cannot forget that agonized, disappointed face our mother could not hide when we were guilty of words or conduct which, to her, were absolutely forbidden. We can never forget her silence, sad eyes, and the slowly formed tear coursing down her cheek.

As Abraham Lincoln once said, "All that I am, or ever hope to be, I owe to my angel mother."

While it is true that we have no choice in the matter of mothers, the great majority of mothers we know have one primary objective in mind for all their children: that they mature to be all they can and should be, lead clean and healthy lives, and fulfill their potential to glorify God.

Mother's Day

Mother's Day

Luke 22:14-20

In 1906 Anna Jarvis was a Sunday school teacher and church organist living in Philadelphia. Her mother died on May 9, 1906 and, ordinarily, her mother's passing would have been mourned only by family and friends. Her death, however, was destined to have an impact far beyond relatives and acquaintances.

Following her mother's death, Anna held a memorial service at her church and asked those attending to wear white carnations, her mother's favorite flower. After the service, Anna learned that many countries had been celebrating Mother's Day since the early 1800's, but the United States had not.

On the first anniversary of her mother's death, Anna asked her church to hold a service in memory of all mothers. The next year, she convinced many church leaders to hold special Mother's Day services near the date of her mother's death. In 1912, Anna organized the Mother's Day International Association, and in 1914, President Woodrow Wilson proclaimed Mother's Day a national observance.

It was Anna Jarvis' great love for her mother that caused her to lead the movement for a national observance of Mother's Day. Because of her efforts, we now set aside the second Sunday

Mark Gambill

in May as a special day to honor our mothers
for their love and sacrifice for us.

Even today, some Americans wear carnations
on Mother's Day, carrying on the tradition
started by Anna Jarvis. Pink carnations honor a
living mother and white carnations symbolize a
mother who has passed away.

Just as the death of Anna Jarvis' mother led
to the institution of Mother's Day, Jesus' death
led to the institution of what we call communion or the Lord's Supper. It is a special time to
focus on His death, burial, and resurrection. A
time to come around His table and commemorate the love He showed to us by carrying our
sins to the cross.

Most of us think of our mothers more often
than just on Mother's Day, and we should
remember Jesus and His great sacrifice for us at
times other than on Sunday morning. It is fit-
ting, however, that we set aside these special
times to honor those to whom honor is due—
our mothers on Mother's Day and Jesus every
Sunday as we meet around His table.

MOTHER'S DAY

NO HALL OF FAME

Exodus 20:12

The fifth Commandment reads, "Honor your father and your mother, so that you may live long in the land the Lord your God is giving you" (Exodus 20:12). God's intention is that parents be loved and honored by their children. Such respect brings stability not only to a family but also to a nation.

Dwight Eisenhower said, "My sainted mother taught me a devotion to God and a love of country which have ever sustained me in my lonely and bitter moments of decision in distant and hostile lands."

There are countless stories about the influence of mothers on their sons and daughters. In the early 40's, a mother struggled to keep her family together after the death of her husband. She worked four jobs: waiting tables in a restaurant, cleaning offices, working at a bakery, and delivering coal in Pittsburgh. Her children learned lessons in persistence and devoted courage from her.

One of her sons wanted to play football, but he was small and slow. When none of the large colleges wanted him, he went to a small college where he played well. He wanted to play professional football, but he was cut from his hometown Steelers. He took a job in construction and

Ward Patterson

played football in a town league for six dollars a game. He wrote countless letters seeking a try-out and was finally given one by the Baltimore Colts. Johnny Unitas is now in the NFL Hall of Fame as one of the greatest quarterbacks ever to play the game.

There is no national hall of fame for mothers, but perhaps there should be—for mothers who set an example of sacrifice, devotion, and practical love—for mothers who modeled courage, patience, and faith—for mothers who taught their children to believe in themselves and to believe in God.

It is unfortunate that in recent years motherhood has lost some of the respect that is due. Women are increasingly encouraged to find their fulfillment outside the home. It is well that there is still a day when the vital role that mothers play is acknowledged and honored.

As we observe Mother's Day, let's remember to be grateful for all faithful mothers, and our own mothers in particular.

MOTHER'S DAY

THE HEART OF A GARDENER

Proverbs 22:6

A gardening book recently pointed out the importance of water in the life of growing plants. They simply can't exist without it. They may have been healthy and well cared for in the nursery, but in your backyard they'll die without a periodic soaking. Without water, plants fail to grow roots. The water has to penetrate deeply enough to cause the tiny roots to reach downward searching it out. A good rule of thumb, we are told, is about an inch of water a week.

The gardening book makes us think about how people are a lot like plants. People need the constant "watering" of encouragement. If they don't get it, they wilt just like dried out marigolds, primroses, or garden peas.

Mothers seem to have been given a talent for "watering" like this. Maybe its because they see their children growing up and attempting new things—a new job, a new investment, a new relationship—and often failing. Some children get depressed and retreat inside themselves, fearful of trying again. It takes a mother's patience and a certain amount of skill to help these children, especially if they resent too much assistance!

Ted Simonson

Mothers know it's often a thankless task to apply a little cheer here, a little comfort there, day after day, until—wonder of wonders!—the first "blossom" of hope and confidence appears!

I suspect that the folks who find themselves doing this kind of work are folks who have tasted loneliness and despair. My guess is that these folks are people who once prayed for help and God sent along one of his "gardeners"— probably a mother—with the "water" of encouragement at just the right time!

If you've got a mother like this, thank the Lord, then "go thou and do likewise."

If you're a mother yourself, ask the Lord for His grace that you might patiently water the plants under your care!

MEMORIAL DAY

1 Corinthians 11:23-26

On the last Monday in May, we celebrate
Memorial Day. Originally, Memorial Day was
called Decoration Day from the practice begun
during the Civil War of decorating the graves of
war dead. An officially set day to decorate the
graves was established in 1868 when General
John Logan, Commander-in-Chief of the Grand
Army of the Republic, issued an order naming
May 30 as a day for "strewing with flowers or
otherwise decorating the graves of comrades
who died in defense of their country during the
late rebellion." As Decoration Day was extended
to include the dead of all wars, it was given the
name Memorial Day.

Memorial Day became a federal holiday in
the late nineteenth century when Congress
noticed that many government employees, who
were veterans, would leave their jobs for the
day, without pay, in order to honor fallen veterans. Memorial Day gives us an occasion to
remember the great sacrifice of these brave
men and women.

A memorial is defined as "something that
keeps remembrance alive." It can be a monu-
ment, keepsake, celebration, or memento. It is a
commemoration of an important person, place,
or event.

Mark Gambill

The apostle Paul in 1 Corinthians 11:23-26 tells us that, "The Lord Jesus, on the night he was betrayed, took bread, and when he had given thanks, he broke it and said, 'This is my body, which is for you; do this in remembrance of me.' In the same way, after supper he took the cup, saying, 'This cup is the new covenant in my blood; do this, whenever you drink it, in remembrance of me.' For whenever you eat this bread and drink this cup, you proclaim the Lord's death until he comes."

In the upper room, Jesus used unleavened bread and a glass of wine and created a memorial that has lasted for two thousand years. The communion service is a weekly reminder of Jesus' death, burial, and resurrection. This celebration keeps alive the great sacrifice Jesus made as He, being without sin, became sin for us, and paid the ultimate price on the cross.

On Memorial Day, we honor the courage of those who died in the service of their country, protecting the freedoms we hold dear. At communion time, we remember the courage of Jesus as He died so that we might have freedom from sin and live with Him eternally. May we never forget the price that was paid for our independence.

MEMORIAL DAY

A VICTORIOUS PERSPECTIVE

1 Corinthians 15:42, 43, 57; Galatians 3:13

Recently, a community cemetery was thoughtlessly ransacked by vandals. Citizens woke up to find tombstones turned over and paint sprayed across mausoleum plaques. Family members of those buried in the cemetery could not understand how anyone could be so cruel and destructive.

Cemeteries play an interesting role in our lives. They mark the graves of our relatives and friends, and they show honor for those who have died defending our national freedom. Every year, millions of Americans visit National Cemeteries for educational purposes, as well as to acknowledge those who have paid the ultimate price. For the majority of the time, however, gravestones stand alone and unnoticed. But when some senseless act dishonors the dead, the names and lives of those long forgotten suddenly find their way back into the public arena.

Similarly, spiritual honor often occurs as a result of dishonor. For example, Christ's greatest triumph followed His apparent defeat at Calvary. Referring to this event, Paul remarked, "Christ redeemed us from the curse of the law by becoming a curse for us, for it is written: 'Cursed is everyone who is hung on a tree'" (Galatians 3:13). Jesus allowed himself to be

Larry Jones

publicly disgraced to conquer the sin and its tragic effect on our lives.

There is also a sense in which our final crown of victory comes only through dishonor. Of death, Paul says, "The body that is sown is perishable, it is raised imperishable; it is sown in dishonor, it is raised in glory; it is sown in weakness, it is raised in power" (1 Corinthians 15:42, 43). From our earthly perspective, death is a curse that separates us from those we love. But from God's perspective, it is a necessary transition that allows us to inherit our eternal reward.

Learn the lesson of the cemetery. Honor sometimes comes through dishonor, victory through defeat, and power through weakness. On Memorial Day, as you remember those who have died, give praise to the One who overcame death through the power of the resurrection. "Thanks be to God! He gives us the victory through our Lord Jesus Christ" (1 Corinthians 15:57).

26

MEMORIAL DAY

A TIME TO REMEMBER

Isaiah 2:3, 4

Memorial Day is a time to remember and contemplate what America and its citizens have lost and gained. Over the span of this nation's history, more than a million soldiers have died in the cause of freedom. Yes, we can put flowers on each grave, count the markers, and adorn the spots with American flags, but we can never count the lost dreams, unfulfilled hopes, and broken hearts caused by so many taken in the bloom of their youth.

Almost two thousand years ago, the matchless Teacher came to earth as angel choirs proclaimed peace on earth and good will toward men. In His teaching He sought to lead us in the way of peace where we might love our enemies and do good to others. Surely by now the churches of Christendom are seeing light enough to begin to walk within the way of the Prince of Peace.

We need to take renewed hope and return to our task of establishing more firmly the house of the Lord, to exalt it above the earthly din so that the nations of the world may say, "Come, let us go up to the mountain of the Lord . . . He will teach us his ways, so that we may walk in his paths." Then "they will beat their swords into plowshares and their spears into pruning

Gladys Smith

hooks. Nation will not take up sword against nation, nor will they train for war anymore" (Isaiah 2:3, 4).

As we rush to meet the demands of our everyday lives, we need to pause for a moment to reflect on what the sacrifice of American lives means. Let us share in a moment of silence as we pay tribute to those no longer with us who gave their all for our freedom. And we need to ask God to deliver us from the delusion that in mighty armies and navies and air power there is a guarantee of peace, and to forgive us for those characteristics and attitudes which tend to make our nation disliked and so greatly feared. And may we each do our utmost to promote world peace by ridding ourselves of prejudice, suspicion, and bitterness toward other races and lands.

On this Memorial Day, let those of us who live in a world of freedom, secured by the sacrifices of so many American lives, take time to remember them, honor them, and exercise with fervency the rights for which they died.

DATE USED _____

58

27

GRADUATION

DON'T SETTLE FOR LESS THAN THE BEST

1 Corinthians 3:21-23

As young people graduate from high school and college, we need to understand that they are going out into a world in which the problems they face will be increasingly difficult. It is a world of politics without principles. It is a world that expects wealth without work. It is a world that enjoys pleasure without conscience. It is a world that practices business without morality. It is a world that attempts to worship without sacrifice. It is a world that applies knowledge without character. It is a world that develops science without compassion. These are the seven deadly sins of our modern culture.

In this difficult world, we wish our graduates the very best. That wish, however, might raise a question regarding what really is best. Many would say that the best things are those that cost the most money, yet there are some things that money cannot buy. For example, money will buy luxury but not culture. Medicine but not health. Sight but not vision. A house but not a home. A bed but not sleep. Insurance but not security. Books but not brains. A church but not a conscience. A cross but not a Savior.

Ross H. Dampier

Therefore, we say, "Don't settle for less than the best. Don't settle for pleasure when you can have happiness. Don't settle for money when you can have wealth. Don't settle for knowledge when you can have wisdom. Don't settle for today when you can have eternity, too."

The apostle Paul tells us in 1 Corinthians 3:21-23 that the person who is in Christ should never accept anything less than the best. He says, "All things are yours, whether Paul or Apollos or Cephas or the world or life or death or the present or the future—all are yours, and you are of Christ, and Christ is of God."

So upon your graduation, we congratulate you, and say to you, "Don't settle for less than the best!"

28

GRADUATION

PRESS ON TO THE GOAL

Psalm 111:10

"What does graduation mean to you?"

That question was asked of five high school seniors and they answered:

"The end of one part of my life and the beginning of another. A feeling of success, but the beginning of more challenges," the first senior said.

"A small stepping stone; the beginning of what I plan to accomplish," added the second senior. "I feel challenged to continue striving toward my goals."

"It's an ending to my childhood. The responsibility for my life, as well as the freedom, will now be mine instead of my parents," the third senior acknowledged.

"I made it!" the fourth senior exclaimed. "I thank the Lord for getting me this far and for His promises to be with me for the rest of my life."

"Since I attended Christian schools, graduation is the final step of a foundation of godly morals from which I can conduct my life," the fifth senior concluded.

There are graduations at many levels— kindergarten, eighth grade, high school, vocational school, college, nurses training, medical school, correspondence school. Each graduation

Judith M. Gonzales

represents a goal the person has met. Each is a milestone.

Graduation is part of a lifelong process of growth. The Bible says, "The fear of the Lord is the beginning of wisdom," (Psalm 111:10). This helps us see that faith in Christ is the only sensible foundation for our lives, and studying Scripture can help us gain knowledge.

Life is full of endings and beginnings, successes and challenges, stepping-stones toward goals. If we accept our responsibilities as well as our freedom at each stage, live thankfully while trusting in God's promises, and build on a godly foundation, we are likely to fit into God's plans for our lives and reach our goals. There can be no greater goal than a personal relationship with Jesus Christ, which means living a life of loving obedience to him as we are empowered by the Holy Spirit to become all He wants us to be.

29

VACATION

WORK, REFLECTION, AND REST

Hebrews 4:9, 10

A woman once overheard another woman say that the very best vacation of her life was the week she spent sitting in a squeaky swing under her backyard shade tree. She did nothing except reflect on the past, take an assessment of the present, and pray about her future.

"I can't remember the last time I felt so refreshed and enlightened," she said. "I returned to work with a peace I'd never had before. My co-workers kept asking what I had done during my vacation that was so exhilarating. I just told them I had spent some quality time with God and it hadn't cost me one cent!"

Whatever your ideal vacation—whether it's like that woman's, or a week spent fishing or camping, or maybe an extended stay in an exotic resort, it can be a time used and dedicated to communicating with God. Taking a break from daily routines and agendas often renews, not only our physical bodies, but our emotional and spiritual being as well. Without the pressures and demands of our usual commitments, we find a sense of freedom and release.

"There remains, then, a Sabbath-rest for the people of God; for anyone who enters God's rest also rests from his own work, just as God

Cheryl Lewis

did from his" (Hebrews 4:9, 10). The writer may have been speaking of the eternal rest we receive after our earthly work is finished, but God also provides and delights in times we dedicate to Him away from our earthly tasks and chores. It simply says to Him that we know there is much more to our living than work, and we are dependent upon Him for renewal and strength.

Reconnecting with God, increasing our faith, gaining new direction for the future, can all be benefits we receive from "rests." God's desire is to speak to us through quietness and peace, without schedules and clocks. The place or activity we choose matters less than our heart's openness. When we allow Him, God can reach us whether we sit beside the ocean or lounge in a tropical setting. He can reach us if we are skiing in the Alps or merely sitting beneath our backyard tree.

30

FATHER'S DAY

FATHER'S DAY

Proverbs 22:6

It has been said that a dad is a fellow who has replaced the money in his wallet with snapshots of his family. No matter where a day takes him or what he does, a dad carries his family in his heart.

Norman Baron tells about his earliest recollection that he has of his father. The two of them were standing waiting for a bus on a cold, wet winter evening when Norman was about four years old. They had been to visit his grandparents and because they had no car, were traveling home by public transportation. To keep Norman warm, his father opened his coat, stood close to Norman, and closed the coat around him. He tells how he felt warm and secure and loved.

Good fathers desire to spend time with their family so they know the family's needs and can do whatever they possibly can to meet those needs. When they laugh with their children, it makes the times of discipline more meaningful. It has been said that the ratio of compliments to discipline should be ninety to ten. That would mean that for every ten times a father needs to discipline a child, he would need to give the child ninety compliments. What a powerful impact on a child to know that one of a father's

Kenneth A. Meade

main goals is to see his children doing what's right and praise them for it. Too often, we may think of a dad only as someone who is looking to find something wrong with a child and disciplining that child for it.

Every father needs to see his son or daughter as someone very special. We need to tell them often that we're glad God gave them to us. It is our desire to not only have a picture of them in our wallets but to always have them in our hearts in a very special place.

Every day a father's prayer should be, "Thank you, Lord, for the privilege and joy of being a father."

31

FATHER'S DAY

JOSEPH

Matthew 1:19, 24; 2:13, 14, 19-21, 22, 23;
Luke 8:19, 20

Of all the great men of the Bible, Joseph, the husband of Mary, must certainly be the most mysterious. We know so little about this man who was chosen by God to function as the father of Jesus.

Scripture tells us that he was a righteous man (Matthew 1:19). He was of good moral character, a man who sought to live according to the commands of God.

Before their marriage, Joseph's attitude toward the pregnant Mary showed kindness and compassion. He had no desire to see her humiliated for what appeared to be her unfaithfulness to him (Matthew 1:19).

He was an obedient man. At least four times an angel gave him instruction in dreams: 1. To wed Mary (Matthew 1:24) 2. To take the young Jesus and Mary to Egypt for their safety (Matthew 2:13, 14) 3. To return to the land of Israel (Matthew 2:19-21) 4. To settle in Galilee (Matthew 2:22, 23). In each instance Joseph was immediate in his obedience, faithful in following God's commands, and content with divine leading.

Luke informs us that Joseph was faithful in offering the appropriate sacrifices in the temple in Jerusalem. Before the arrival of the wise men, he

Ward Patterson

and Mary took Jesus to Jerusalem to "present him to the Lord." As Jesus was growing up, his parents observed the Passover every year in Jerusalem.

We know little else about this remarkable man. We know that he and Mary had children after the birth of Jesus (Luke 8:19, 20). We know that he was a carpenter. We know that he and Mary took Jesus to Jerusalem when he was twelve years old.

Then Joseph disappears from the narrative. There is no mention of sickness or death. He merely does his best in rearing Jesus. And then he is gone.

We are left to surmise a few things about him and his role in training Jesus. He must have been a loving and kind father to Jesus. Jesus urged His followers to think of God as their heavenly Father. "Father" was a word that was warm and rich to Jesus, doubtless because the man chosen to serve as His earthly father filled that role with grace and love.

The life of Joseph has a message for all men who are entrusted with the lives of young men and women. Your character is of paramount importance. Seek righteousness. Be kind and compassionate. Be obedient to God, taking His commands very seriously. Be faithful in worship. Set an example in your work and in your home.

OUR FATHER

Mark 14:36; John 14:8; Romans 8:15; Galatians 4:6

The headline read "Forty Year Wait to Meet Father." The story that followed was that of a woman who had been separated from her father when she was a baby. Becoming curious she began a long and painful search that at last brought father and daughter together.

For us all there is a similar longing with regard to our heavenly Father. Philip spoke for us all when he said, "Show us the Father and that will be enough for us" (John 14:8). Thomas Wolfe said it seemed to him that the thing that was central to all living was man's search for a Father. It was not, he explained, the lost father of his youth, but a power external to his need.

So, Father's Day is a good time to think about the God whom Jesus taught us to call "our Father." No one ever addressed God in that way before Jesus. True, he is described before as being like a father, but to address him directly as father is something that began with Jesus. Right away, of course, we must know that God is not like any other father who ever lived. If one's father was easygoing and good-natured, one is apt to think that God takes little account of evil. If one's father was autocratic, unyielding

Robert C. Shannon

69

and unforgiving, one is apt to think of God in those terms. So we must always remember that God is not like your father or my father or any other father who ever lived. He is the father of our Lord Jesus Christ and is unique just as Jesus was unique. Still it is useful to know that we belong to the same spiritual family as our Lord Jesus Christ and we can call God, "Father." Both Jesus and the apostle Paul used the more intimate and informal and family term, "Abba, Father," (Mark 14:36; Romans 8:15; Galatians 4:6).

The nearest we can come to that in English is "Daddy." Certainly no one would suggest that we call God, Daddy. That title has been misused too much in the world of entertainment to use it of God. But it does help us understand that our relationship to God is as close and intimate as any we experience. He is that kind of Father. The best kind of Father.

THE ROLE OF FATHER

Ephesians 5:23; 6:4

He is known by many names—Father, Dad, Papa, Pappy, or Pa. He has a varied and multi-faceted role in the life of a family. He is the family provider, head of the house, father of the family, priest of the home, mender of toys, the mover of couches, the pounder of nails, remover of trash, raker of leaves, hanger of screens, and so much more. He is the behind-the-scenes person. Mother is the heart of the family and father is the head.

Paul Harvey says, "A father is a thing forced to endure childbirth without an anesthetic. He is never quite the hero his daughter thinks, never quite the man his son believes him to be, and this worries him sometimes."

God ordains a father to be the physical, spiritual, and emotional head of the family. "For the husband is the head of the wife as Christ is the head of the church" (Ephesians 5:23).

Ephesians 6:4 says, "Fathers . . . bring them [children] up in the training and instruction of the Lord."

Mrs. John Bruce Dodd of Spokane, Washington, suggested the idea of Father's Day to honor her father, William Smart, a veteran of the War between the States. Her father had

Jean P. Sours

reared his six motherless children on an eastern Washington farm.

William Jennings Bryan was one of the first to give endorsement to Mrs. Dodd's plan. And in 1924, President Calvin Coolidge recommended a national observance of Father's Day.

A father is God's representative to his children. This makes a father's task sacred and serious. A father is to deal with his children as God deals with the him as God's child. The heavenly Father is seen in the eyes and hearts of children as they watch their earthly father. The role of father is awesome.

Fathers sometimes find it difficult to say, "I love you," but they need to hear those words. As we honor our fathers today, let's remember to thank them, say "I love you," and be grateful for the awesome role they play in our lives.

Giving them a hug would be nice, too!

INDEPENDENCE DAY

34

JULY 4TH

Galatians 5:13, 14

From the perspective of our own national history, no date is more significant than this—the Fourth of July—or, as we often say, "Independence Day."

Do you remember the first time you heard the thrilling story of our nation's birth in freedom from the burdensome levies against English citizens in this new world? The story should be a source of gratitude and give us deep respect for those who bought this freedom with their blood!

Independence Day! Exciting! A story we teach to our children, and our children's children.

Our liberties have been threatened numerous times, from outside and inside as well. We are rightly warned that "eternal vigilance is the price of liberty," and it is so.

If this is true in the national scene, it is equally true in the individual Christian's life. We cannot always know when or in what manner Satan will toss one of his soul-endangering curves at us. It may come from a friend, from a stranger, or, as we have been warned, our foes may arise from among those of our own household! In spiritual living, as well as in political

Brant Lee Doty

circumstances, we must be constantly on the alert.

As Americans, we should daily renew our commitment to freedom—both ours and our neighbors. At the same time, we must not endanger our personal liberties through selfish, inconsiderate, or sinful conduct. When we seek only our own welfare, or intrude upon the freedom of others, we lose an even greater freedom, the freedom to become all that God wants us to be, or to do all He asks of us.

If we fail to commit to freedom—both ours and our neighbors—we lose freedom from sin, and we gain an accusing conscience.

35

INDEPENDENCE DAY

THEY PLEDGED THEIR ALL

Matthew 26:28; Luke 9:22

No doubt you've heard of the Declaration of Independence, but have you read it? To me, the most important line in the Declaration says, "For the support of this declaration, with a firm reliance on the protection of the Divine Providence, we mutually pledge to each other, our lives, our fortunes, and our sacred honor," because that's where the signers promised, "We're going to put our money (and lives) where our mouth is." And they did.

History records that nine of the signers were killed in the Revolutionary War. Five more were tortured by the British. Two lost their sons in the war and another two had sons captured. A dozen or more had their homes pillaged and burned by the Redcoats. Their lives, and deaths, testify to their commitment to the Declaration.

Richard Stockton, a New Jersey State Supreme Court Justice, was arrested by British troops, thrown into jail, and nearly starved to death. After his release, he found that his estate had been looted and burned. He died before the war's end, leaving his family in poverty.

John Hart, a New Jersey farmer, had to leave behind his wife and thirteen children when the British came for him. He lived on the run for over a year, hiding in forests and sleeping in

Richard Koffarnus

caves. When he finally returned home, he discovered that his wife had died, his children were gone, and his farm was destroyed. He died in 1779, never having found his lost children.

Brave words backed by brave deeds, remind us of our Lord Jesus. Remember when He pledged, "The Son of Man must suffer many things and be rejected by the elders, chief priests and teachers of the law, and he must be killed and on the third day be raised to life" (Luke 9:22)? And again, at the last supper, "This is my blood of the covenant, which is poured out for many for the forgiveness of sins" (Matthew 26:28)? Then Jesus went out and kept His promise, allowing himself to be crucified so that you and I might have salvation.

The signers of the Declaration were willing to give their lives to secure liberty for themselves and their country, but Jesus was willing to do even more. He died for a cause that was not just right; it was essential. He died not just for political freedom but for eternal life. He died not with the support of a grateful nation, but alone, suspended on a cross. And He did it for you and me.

36

INDEPENDENCE DAY

ONE DEATH LEADS TO LIBERTY

James 1:27

Who can forget the emotional cry, "Give me liberty or give me death!" Patrick Henry broadcast this call to arms on March 23, 1775, when he asked the Virginia Convention: "Is life so dear or peace so sweet as to be purchased at the price of chains and slavery?"

Those who fought against tyranny in the American Revolution wanted to form a government that guaranteed the inalienable rights of people granted by their creator. On the Fourth of July, we celebrate the signing of the Declaration of Independence, a document whose signers committed themselves to fighting for political liberty. With firm resolve these men led many to sacrifice and die that we might be free.

Most signers of the Declaration of Independence were followers of Jesus and one was a minister. They knew that the sacrificial death of one man, Jesus Christ, made possible the spiritual liberty of people from every tribe, tongue, and nation. Jesus fought and defeated Satan, temptation, and death so those who followed him could be freed from Satan's tyranny. The shed blood of Jesus cleanses His followers' conscience and frees them from bondage to sin. His Spirit empowers Christians to fight evil and

L. G. Parkhurst, Jr.

overcome temptations in every arena of life. By His death and resurrection, Jesus enables many to gain spiritual liberty and eternal life.

George Washington and the other American patriots did not fight for our liberty so we could live in selfish unconcern. They fought to establish the rule of law with the consent of the governed. Jesus Christ freed his followers from spiritual tyranny so they could hear and do the Word of God. Through an active faith in Him, they can bring happiness to God and others. The Bible teaches that the perfect law of liberty for Christians is loving God and our neighbors, even our enemies. Such love seeks the best for others in every way it wisely can. God's love empowers us to do good, to help those in distress, and to keep ourselves "from being polluted by the world" (James 1:27). Patrick Henry emphasized that, "it is the mutual duty of all to practice Christian forbearance, love, and charity towards each other."

And on this 4th of July, we give thanks for Patrick Henry, George Washington, and the many nameless patriots who suffered and died that we Americans might be free.

37

INDEPENDENCE DAY

OUR COUNTRY'S BIRTHDAY

Isaiah 55:10, 11

As we celebrate the birthday of our country, we remember how the early settlers fought terrible conditions in order to gain freedom to worship God. They were blessed for their loyalty to God. During the Revolutionary War, one particular battle shows God's obvious assistance.

In August of 1776, a British fleet of two hundred ships brought thirty thousand troops to the Brooklyn area. The Battle of Long Island was disastrous to the patriots. Washington's army was defeated and would have been destroyed except for Divine intervention. The patriots were pinned down with the British army in front and the mile wide East river behind. General Washington was afraid that the British fleet would travel up the river and completely cut off all means of retreat as well as capturing the army. The General started moving his troops across the river leaving a front line so the British wouldn't suspect a retreat was occurring. About dawn, there were three regiments still on duty. A dense fog began to rise. It was so thick, the militia could see no farther than six yards away. The fog remained most of the day which allowed the entire army to be ferried across the river to safety.

Jo Stolle

God remains in control of our country though we do not often see miracles of this magnitude. Our greatest need was granted through His Son. Our forefathers fought for the privilege to settle in this country where they could worship God freely. They knew our Christian freedom was not cheap but was purchased with the blood of the Lord Jesus Christ. God sent Jesus to earth to be that final sacrifice, which would provide the way of salvation for us—the ultimate freedom. In this time, God has not left us to fend for ourselves.

Isaiah 55:10, 11 says, "As the rain and the snow come down from heaven, and do not return to it without watering the earth and making it bud and flourish, so that it yields seed for the sower and bread for the eater, so is my word that goes out from my mouth: It will not return to me empty, but will accomplish what I desire and achieve the purpose for which I sent it."

Remember what God has done for us in Jesus and pray for God's continued guidance in our country.

LABOR DAY

38

ON LABOR DAY

Genesis 3:17-19

The very term *labor* can have a very negative connotation—that of strenuous and often unwelcome exertion. Webster's first definition is "expenditure of physical or mental effort, esp. when difficult or compulsory." A later added thought: "to exert one's powers of body or mind, esp. with painful or strenuous effort: WORK." Sounds a little like God's pronouncement upon Adam (Genesis 3:17-19), that his livelihood would come "by the sweat of his brow," doesn't it?

Although modern machinery performs many of the more arduous tasks we require to earn a livelihood, we cannot simply let nature take its course to produce its food-bounty without tilling, sowing, cultivating, and reaping. Ask any contemporary farmer who operates the big tractor pulling a gang plow, or other essential implements for cultivation, planting, weeding, or harvesting, and he will not hesitate to term his expenditure of energy as work.

And there is an abundance of tasks to which we apply ourselves with laborious intensity in earning a livelihood. Those who sit all day at a desk solving difficult problems, resolving dilemmas, preparing complex and intricate schedules, surely qualify as workers! Intense, precise

Brant Lee Doty

81

mental exertion may induce weariness as certainly as physical stress; and rest, relaxation, or a change of activity is the appropriate prescription for recovery.

Our work, then, may be less physically strenuous than that of our forefathers, but we have a valid claim to "earning our bread by the sweat of our brows," have we not?

Let it then also be said that all of our labors should be concerned with these consequences: the fruits of the labor should be in proportion to the exertion required; the task itself should be worth the doing; the honest laborer deserves an honest wage; and we should share the fruits of our labor with those unable to provide for themselves or are victims of catastrophic events. We must remember that in all things, it is God himself who will be the judge of the fruit and consequences of all our labors. Let them be done, then, in His manner, and to His glory.

39

LABOR DAY

YOUR LABOR OF LOVE

Matthew 25:40; 1 Corinthians 10:31; 15:58

"Service with a smile," though a slogan of many businesses, is difficult to live out in daily life. How can we smile if the only reason we are serving is to pay bills at the end of the month? Working to feed and clothe our families can become monotonous when we feel as though we are spending more time on the job than we are able to spend at home enjoying our families. Even employment that challenges our minds or provides opportunities for career advancement does not always bring the reward we truly seek.

Though employment fulfills certain expectations, God designed a greater satisfaction for our daily service. God desires us to work for Him. "Therefore, my dear brothers, stand firm. Let nothing move you. Always give yourselves fully to the work of the Lord, because you know that your labor in the Lord is not in vain" (1 Corinthians 15:58).

Though many well-meaning employees can give service with a smile because it is their duty, only employees who are serving God through their vocations can smile because they have a joyful heart. God's standards of service are high, it is true, but He promises to give us joy when we serve out of our love for Him. Whether the

Lisa Lehman

job is menial labor or in executive status, God expects His servants to serve Him with a smile. "So whether you eat or drink or whatever you do, do it all for the glory of God" (1 Corinthians 10:31).

What is your labor of love? What do you do daily because you love God?

When a customer asks for a refill of water (or soft drink or coffee), God says we are to give Him a drink. When a co-worker interrupts our meeting with an urgent phone call, God asks us to listen to Him. And when our children ask us to read the same dog-eared book that we read carefully an hour earlier, God desires that we repeat the story for His enjoyment. Whether you give of yourself in the home or in the office, at the school or at the hospital, give your best to the Lord. Serve God with a smile, and you will find joy in your labor.

"The king will reply, 'I tell you the truth, whatever you did for one of the least of these brothers of mine, you did for me'" (Matthew 25:40).

40

GRANDPARENT'S DAY

BECOMING GREAT GRANDPARENTS

Galatians 6:7

In recent years we have seen increasing emphasis on Grandparent's Day. What a wonderful time of life it is when we become grandparents! How we look forward to it, and when it comes, how we enjoy it. We should remember, however, that becoming a grandparent is something that just happens naturally, but being a really good grandparent takes years of preparation. Have you thought about the kind of person you will be when you are old enough to be a grandparent?

Someday you are going to meet an old person. Down the road, ten, twenty, thirty years from now, that person is waiting for you. What kind of person will you be then? Will you be a kind and generous individual surrounded by friends and relatives, the kind of person who is everybody's grandma or grandpa? Will you be a bitter, disillusioned, cynical old grouch who doesn't have a good word for anybody and is alone all the time?

The kind of person you will meet down the road depends entirely on you, because that person is you. You will be a composite of everything that you think and say and do today. That person will be exactly as you make him. Nothing more and nothing less.

Ross H. Dampier

a
time to
speak

Every day and in every way you are becoming more like yourself. You look more like yourself; you think more like yourself; you talk more like yourself. Live selfishly and the old person will get smaller, harder, crabbier, crustier. Live more for others and that person will become softer, sweeter, kinder, and more gentle.

We make the mistake of thinking that one day it will all happen quite naturally. Someday our children will have children and we will be grandparents. If we are to be really great grandparents, we must make the best use of our opportunities every day. At any given moment, you are the sum total of your life up till then. There are no big events which we can reach unless we have built a pile of smaller moments to stand on. If we are to be effective grandparents we must remember what the apostle Paul said in Galatians 6:7, "Do not be deceived: God cannot be mocked. A man reaps what he sows."

Let's start today getting ready to be great grandparents.

41

GRANDPARENT'S DAY

GRANDPARENT'S DAY

2 Timothy 1:5

To the uninitiated the difference between a parent and a grandparent may seem obscure, but to the participants in these relationships the distinctions are very real. From the Old Testament to the New, holy Scripture constantly emphasizes the divine institution of the home and defines for us the unique roles of parents and grandparents. For the parent, responsibility, example, and loving discipline stand out as lessons to be taught in the formative years of the child's life. For grandparents, confirmation, reinforcement, and graceful aging seem foremost in the contributions they make to their grandchildren.

Second Timothy 1:5 recognizes the ability of a grandparent, Lois, to reinforce the teaching and living example of her daughter, Eunice, to her grandson, Timothy. Eunice, a Jewess, evidently was married to a Gentile (Greek) husband who gave no discernible spiritual assistance in the rearing of Timothy. But Eunice had the great assistance of her godly mother in the teaching of the holy Scripture to him.

Many of the Old Testament characters lived to be grandfathers and grandmothers, and their influence in confirming the validity of God's

James W. Dyer

teaching in Scripture was probably of great value to their grandchildren.

Perhaps the greatest contribution we grandparents can give our family is that of growing old gracefully. Again, it is the Scripture that gives us, as grandparents, lessons to teach and examples to live by, as we strive to help today's Christian young people grow in their faith.

We often hear folks rejoicing in the great numbers of young people in a particular church. But the only way to ensure the passing on of the faith is to have a church with senior adults whose lives are living proof that God's Word and God's church are powerful weapons in keeping bright the promise of eternal joy in God's presence.

42

GRANDPARENT'S DAY

GOOD GRANDPARENTS

Proverbs 22:6

Myron and Mary Ben Madden suggest in *For Grandparents: Wonders and Worries* that, "Grandparents who know how to back off when circumstances warrant, are truly a gift. They are of special help when they can be available but not pushy, on call but not always present, helpful but not obvious."

Are you aware that it's often hard work learning how to be a good grandparent? It doesn't just happen! We have to remember that our grandchildren have parents who are primarily in charge and grandparents are secondary. Grandparents have to learn to work in harmony with parents so grandchildren do not receive mixed messages on what is right and wrong.

A question grandparents should often ask parents is, "Do you mind if the grandchildren...?" This question can help grandparents avoid what happened to a certain grandmother one time. She didn't listen when the parents clearly let it be known that they did not want their young child to have a drum at his age. At Christmas, the grandmother went ahead and bought the drum. Of course, the little guy was really happy when he started pounding on it right after he opened his gift at Grandma's house. The wise

Kenneth A. Meade

parents responded, "Josh, that's a very special gift from Grandma. We're going to leave it here at Grandma's house so it'll always be here when you come to visit and you can play your beautiful drum music which I'm sure Grandma will really love." We smile at such a subtle way of handling a difficult situation but it speaks volumes to us as grandparents.

Grandparents have spent a great deal of time loving and giving to family. Now, it is time for family to find creative and innovative ways to give to them as an expression of gratitude. By nature, most grandparents love to give. By the time they become grandparents, it makes giving even more meaningful when the family realizes how important it is to give the grandparents themselves, not only gifts, but time to be with the family. We're all aware how quickly time is passing by.

There is a bumper sticker that reads, "If I'd known how much fun it would be to have grandchildren, I'd have had them first." Of course, that is not a choice. But, we can hope and pray we are all loved and appreciated as children, parents, and grandparents.

43

THANKSGIVING

THANKSGIVING IS NOT A DAY

Psalm 7:17

Thanksgiving is not a day. It is a way of life.

It is the feeling you get when you sit down to supper after a hard day's work and you are grateful that your "tired" is a healthy tired. It is looking at the sunset after a hot bright day of travel and knowing that today you have not had to walk alone. It is looking at harvested fields and autumn-bright leaves and knowing that God did that, too.

Thanksgiving is having a job. It is the privilege of not being misunderstood when you grumble about having to go to work, while at the same time you are deeply grateful that you have health and strength and a job to do.

Thanksgiving is living in a country where you are free. It is knowing that you do not have to wait for a presidential proclamation, but that you can say, "Thank God," every day because of religious liberty.

Thanksgiving is not just a table spread with turkey and trimmings and half a hundred relatives gathered 'round. It is a kitchen table and a checkered cloth and Mom and Dad and soup beans and cornbread and milk. It is a couple of wiggly kids who are quiet for a moment as we say, "God is great," in unison.

Ross H. Dampier

Sometimes Thanksgiving is sitting in a hospital room when a loved one is sick and knowing that God is there, too. It is the preacher coming to say a quiet prayer. It is the feeling of assurance when doctors and nurses are nearby. It is the cards and flowers and kind words of those who care enough to send the very best—their own deep love and concern.

Thanksgiving is meeting with your friends at church. It is the reading of God's Word; it is the voice of the choir; it is a bit of bread and a sip of wine; it is a whispered prayer, in Jesus' name, amen.

Thanksgiving is people making it together with God's help. It is old friends and the understanding of the years. It is new friends and the anticipation of the future. It is old folks and young folks, and good days and bad days, and past and future, all together.

Thanksgiving is not a day. It is the way you live your life!

44

THANKSGIVING

THANKING GOD FOR GRACE

Ephesians 1:3-23

As two small children played together, the host mother brought in a tray filled with apple wedges and peanut butter crackers. The visiting child bowed his head in prayer but was interrupted by his playmate's curiosity when he asked, "What are you doing?"

"Thanking God for the snack," said the youngster nonchalantly.

"You don't thank God for snacks, silly" the friend giggled, "you wait for the big food!"

Let's face it. If it weren't for a day such as Thanksgiving, not many of us would spend deliberate time in reflection and praise about the goodness of God. Waiting for special days, we overlook His daily sustaining power and tend to focus on the tangible, physical miracles and gifts.

The little boy in our story had developed an excellent habit—one of giving thanks for things too often counted as insignificant and ordinary.

The apostle Paul's words in the first chapter of Ephesians bring comfort to all believers. We are chosen. Redeemed. Forgiven. Rich with love and wisdom and grace. Whether we gather with others or spend this time alone. Whether our health is good, or we are enduring some illness. Regardless of our financial situation, we

Cheryl Lewis

can give thanks because God's gifts are not dependent upon our circumstances. He has chosen us to be His—for now and through eternity.

So, too, our Savior's gifts come nestled between the common and the awesome—for these we give thanks. Perhaps today, as we count our blessings, we can add laughter and peace of mind. Renewed faith and joy. We can add courage and hope and the privilege of sharing our Savior's heavenly home. We can pray, as did the little boy, for simple fare or feasts, for the steadfastness given every day, and the Savior's wonderful grace.

45

THANKSGIVING

THANKSGIVING

Exodus 23:14-16; Philippians 4:6

Today, on this national holiday, we carry on the tradition of thanksgiving to God that the pilgrims first celebrated in 1621. Governor William Bradford of the Plymouth Colony had proclaimed it a day of special thanksgiving. After a long, hard winter, the pilgrims prepared wild turkeys, among other foods, to share with the other colonists and the neighboring Indians.

The first national Thanksgiving Day, November 26, 1789, was proclaimed by George Washington and is celebrated today. We also invite friends and relatives to visit. We prepare turkey, mashed potatoes, sweet potatoes, rutabaga, salad, ethnic foods, and many desserts. The turkey is not the only one that gets stuffed!

Thanksgiving, however, didn't begin with pilgrims in America but with the Israelites, God's people, a long time ago. In the Old Testament we read about all the laws God gave His people, but He also gave them feasts. These feasts were to be celebrations of His goodness to them. He had delivered His chosen people by direct intervention and the people were grateful. God told them to keep the Feast of Unleavened Bread, the Feast of Harvest, and the

Kathleen A. Thompson

Feast of Ingathering to remind them of His goodness (Exodus 23:14-16).

The Feast of Harvest was also called the Feast of Weeks and the Day of First Fruits. Later this became known as Pentecost. God wanted the Israelites to enjoy the fruits of their labor and also to be thankful for them.

In the New Testament, Paul tells us in his letter to the Philippians: "Do not be anxious about anything, but in everything, by prayer and petition, with thanksgiving, present your requests to God" (4:6). It is good to share and to enjoy what we have but let's not limit our thankfulness to one day. Let's be thankful every day of the year. Our faith grows as we pray to God with thanksgiving.

46

THANKSGIVING

GIVING THANKS

Luke 1:46, KJV

We live in a worldly culture. The holidays rich in spiritual significance have been made paltry and meaningless in the world's eyes. New Year's Day has become the day of Super Bowls and hangovers. Valentine's Day no longer commemorates a loving saint but is a day to exchange mushy, expensive cards and high-calorie candy. Good Friday and Easter are the backdrop for the Easter bunny. The 4th of July is the day to set off hundreds of dollars of fireworks, and Christmas is a high-stress holiday with dozens and dozens of presents to buy, a time of year to go financially berserk with a credit card.

And in the meantime, the real meaning of these special days is too often forgotten or ignored. That has become true even with Thanksgiving, now commonly known as Turkey Day. The first Thanksgiving came with a ferocious price and was celebrated by pilgrims who had left absolutely everything behind—family, friends, all security and ease. But that first winter, they did not commemorate their hardships but their great gratitude to God for His provision and care.

Giving thanks binds the heart of the receiver with the heart of the giver. As our capacity to

Maria Anne Tolar

give thanks to God increases, so does our knowledge of Him. Mary said, "My soul doth magnify the Lord" (Luke 1:46, KJV). Our ability to thank our Lord and Savior is a special key, enabling us to see Him more clearly. We enter His courts with thanksgiving in our hearts, come into His presence with praise. Giving thanks ushers our prayers into His presence. We can't praise Him if we don't know Him; we can't thank Him if we don't discern Him.

The pilgrims are forever a part of our heritage, not just because they were brave enough to travel to this new land but because their souls magnified the Lord. When they barely had anything that first year, they still had much more than enough to declare a day of thanksgiving.

We have a wonderful heritage to treasure. Let us give endless thanks to the same blessed Lord God that our forefathers revered and worshiped.

47

CHRISTMAS

THE GIFTS OF THE MAGI

Matthew 2:1-12

A favorite Christmas story is "Gift of the Magi" by O. Henry. The story concerns a young married couple, Jim and Della Young. The Youngs have fallen on tough times and neither Jim nor Della has the money to buy a suitable Christmas present for the other. As the story unfolds, we find that Della's most prized possession is her beautiful, knee-length brown hair, and Jim's is a gold watch, a family heirloom. To get Jim a gift worthy of her love for him, Della trades her tresses for twenty dollars and buys Jim a platinum fob chain for his splendid watch. In a wonderfully ironic ending that is classic O. Henry, Della and Jim exchange gifts on Christmas Eve, only to find that Jim has sold his watch to buy Della a set of beautiful tortoise shell combs for her hair. Though the world would consider them foolish, O. Henry calls Della and Jim the wisest of all who give gifts. They willingly, lovingly sacrificed for each other their greatest treasures—they are the magi.

When you think about it, O. Henry's story has much in common with Matthew's account of the magi. First, like Jim and Della, the wise men sacrificed much—their wealth, their time, their safety—to give Jesus their most precious gifts. And in return, Jesus willingly sacrificed

Richard Koffarnus

all—His comfort, His place in Heaven, His very life—to bring them the most precious of all gifts, eternal life.

Second, Herod undoubtedly scoffed at the magi's selfless act of generosity, just as the world laughed at Jim and Della. So what? Earthly values have never been able to comprehend heavenly wisdom. Only those with minds set on things above would understand such sacrificial giving.

Third, there is even a touch of irony worthy of O. Henry in Matthew's story. The magi who came to worship Jesus unwittingly put His life in jeopardy, then, just as unwittingly, provided Joseph and Mary with the means to flee to safety. Never underestimate God's power to turn a crisis into a happy ending.

Of course, there is one key difference between the two stories: one is fiction and the other is fact. Jesus really lived and died and lived again to give us life eternal. And the magi really worshiped Him, as you and I should. That's why O. Henry's tale makes great reading, but Matthew's is the greatest story ever told.

48

CHRISTMAS

CHRISTMAS

John 3:16

On a Sunday, December 25, motorists in Fort Myers, Florida, who received police department parking tickets, were pleasantly surprised at the message on them. The tickets read: "You have been caught. All is forgiven. Best wishes and a Merry Christmas from the Police Department." The police felt justified in granting forgiveness on the day that the world celebrates as the birth of Him through whom, alone, real forgiveness can be obtained.

The worshiping of Christ began in Bethlehem centuries ago by angels and has been continued down through the ages by followers of Christ. Decorations and gifts to others are but ways of bringing happiness to our friends. It is possible, however, for us to be celebrating Christmas without focusing on the true meaning.

The Bible tells us, "God so loved the world that he gave his one and only Son, that whoever believes in him shall not perish but have eternal life" (John 3:16). That is the true message of Christmas. Christ was born and came to earth so that we might be forgiven.

Isn't it a wonderful feeling to have someone say, "I forgive you"? People don't have to forgive us. God didn't have to forgive us. People choose to forgive us. God chooses to forgive us. If you

Kenneth A. Meade

listen carefully, you can almost hear the voice of God saying, "Merry Christmas, you are forgiven. Have a great day and a happy new year!"

There are so many conflicting stories about where the idea of Santa Claus originated. It seems that no one really knows. But, we know that Jesus came from God. Jesus died for us. We are forgiven. Knowing this, and having accepted Jesus as our Lord and Savior, we can truly have a Merry Christmas.

We shouldn't park illegally. But, if we did, wouldn't it be nice sometime to get a note like the one left by the police department in Fort Myers, Florida?

But we all can say, "Thank you, God, for Jesus. Merry Christmas!"

49

CHRISTMAS

THE GEORGE BAILEY TEST

John 3:16

You could call it the "George Bailey Test." You remember George Bailey, of course. He's the hero of "It's a Wonderful Life," which you can find on TV at this time of year. George's struggle to better the lot of his fellowman seems to have been for nothing. Clarence the angel appears and shows George how bad things would've been if he had never been born. George gets the message, begs for his life back and goes on a wiser, happier man.

Does the world seem dark and dreary? Are you close to despair? When life seems nothing more than "a tale told by an idiot, full of sound and fury, signifying nothing," (Shakespeare) ask yourself this question: "What if He had never been born?" Not George Bailey but Jesus Christ!

If Jesus hadn't been born, what then? No cross, no tomb, no resurrection. If Jesus had never walked this earth, what then? No disciples, no church, no fellowship. Sure, the drugs still flow and the guns are heard in the night, but how many have been pulled from the gutter because of Jesus? How many have been rescued from meaninglessness, purposelessness, and despair? Yes, the world can be a scary place, but just think how much worse if Jesus had never been born!

Gary D. Robinson

Think about it. If Jesus had never been born, where would the love, the goodness, the meaning have come from? Would we even be alive? Would life without Jesus be worth living at all? If we track the possibility of Jesus having never been born, the trail leads to a cliff above a terrifying abyss! We scream, "Get me back! I want to live again!"

Need a reason to celebrate on the twenty-fifth of December, or the twenty-fifth of July? Try the "George Bailey Test."

50

CHRISTMAS

HAPPY BIRTHDAY

Matthew 2:1, 2

How would you answer if you were asked by a roving reporter to give your opinion of history's most important happening? I've heard this happened one day on the streets of New York City, and people's answers were varied, revealing their prejudices. One said the invention of the wheel, others mentioned the defeat of the Muslims by the English, the settling of Jamestown by the British, the defeat of Hitler, or the splitting of the atom.

But a thirteen-year-old school boy's opinion was, "the birth of Jesus Christ." And though Advent and Christmas are to honor that pivotal time in history, the world often crowds Him out.

God chose the natural birth of a baby to reveal the spiritual truth of a Savior. And Heaven announced His arrival—angels with heavenly songs and shepherds appearing at the stable to worship the newborn King. God chose the natural—a star—to guide the wise men from the East, and their encounter with the spiritual changed their lives.

The world was ready for a redeemer. The Israelites had returned from captivity in Babylon. And Greek and Roman culture brought a common language, democracy, and a

Dorothy N. Snyder

road system for expansion. Christ's coming ful-
filled the Old Testament prophecies of the
Messiah who would save the world from the
tragedy of its sins. It also unveiled the mystery
of a new relationship between God and man.
Jesus' teachings often used the realities of
nature to illustrate a spiritual truth. His death
and resurrection forever changed and empowered His followers of all ages to rise above the
powers that could defeat them.

The question of the ages continues: "Where
is He?" Sometimes it is hard to find Him among
the glitter and sparkles, the Santa Clauses, and
the dollar signs. Have we allowed the explosion
of science and technology to temporarily eclipse
the power of the One born in the manger—
Immanuel?

We can join the young boy who thought
Jesus' birth was all-important. There's a glory
and a wonder and a beauty to Advent. Let's
bow before the manger and let the kernel of
Christmas explode in our midst. It's His birthday we celebrate! Happy birthday, Lord Jesus!

51

MISSIONS

STEWARDSHIP MEDITATION

Matthew 25:45, KJV

An Englishman had often boasted that he did not believe in God. One day his travels took him to the Fiji Islands. While there, he witnessed the natives attending church with their Bibles in their hands.

As he watched them go by he called out, "The Bible is no good. Your religion about Christ is false."

A simple native teacher heard the Englishman's charge and answered him, "It is a good thing for you that we left our heathenism and cannibalism and took to our Bibles and Christianity, else you would by now have been clubbed, cooked in a pot, and eaten!"

These and thousands of other such testimonies establish the fact that the gospel of Christ brings about change and impacts the world for good. When we sacrificially give to support missions, we are making it possible for individuals as well as whole cultures to be blessed by the difference that Christ can make.

There has never been a time when missions was more vital than today. As Arden Almquist wrote in *Missionary Come Back:* "Africa is at a time of decision. A hundred million animists in Africa alone will decide in our lifetime whether to become Christian, Muslim, or agnostic."

Arthur O. Peterson II

DATE USED _____

David Livingstone put it very simply: "God had an only Son, and He was a missionary and a physician." A contemporary of Livingstone was Henry Martyn, a pioneer preacher in India. Martyn laid down this axiom of missions: "The Spirit of Christ is the spirit of missions, and the nearer we get to Him the more intensely missionary we must become."

In too many churches the emphasis on missions is conspicuously absent. Sadly, giving to the work of missions has become optional rather than expected. As a result, the mission field and the work that needs to be done suffers from neglect. Missionaries become beggars and this work of the church that should be given emphasis becomes minimized.

Horace Bushnell once made an interesting list of all who might be excused from giving to missions. The last on his list of those to be excused were those who are prepared to accept the final sentence: "Inasmuch as ye did it not to one of the least of these, ye did it not to me" (Matthew 25:45, KJV).

Let's give generously toward missions. Remember that God had one Son and He was a missionary!

52

MISSIONS

WHITE UNTO HARVEST

1 Corinthians 3:6

Many years ago a young man heard a missionary sermon based on Jesus' words to "look on the fields; for they are white already to harvest." He was so impressed by the sermon that he made a commitment to become a missionary. The young man spent several years in college and special training to prepare himself for mission work. He eventually felt called to a mission field where no other missionary had ever worked before. He spent many years there in diligent work, but the many years of effort brought very meager returns in terms of converts. In his old age he returned to his home town a disappointed man because the white harvests that the preacher had promised years before had not materialized.

After returning home, the missionary went to visit a boyhood friend, a successful farmer who had provided considerable financial support for him. He felt compelled to apologize to his old friend because he had so little to show for all his efforts and for the money that had been spent in a seemingly futile effort.

The farmer listened to his story and then offered him words of sympathy. "My friend," he said, "look out across my fields. They are indeed white unto harvest, but those fields have not always looked that way. My great grandfather homesteaded this very land over a hundred years ago, but then it was a

John W. Wade

dense forest. He had to spend most of his life clearing the trees, and he was barely able to grow enough to keep his family alive. Then my grandfather took over the farm. He cleared out the stumps and rocks and made the fields more fruitful. Then my father took over the farm. He put in drainage ditches and terraces that made the fields even more fruitful. Then the farm became mine. I introduced scientific farming that involved crop rotation, hybrid seeds, fertilizers, and irrigation. As a result my fields are much more productive than the same fields were when they were farmed by my ancestors. Did it ever occur to you that God called you to that mission field, not to reap the harvest, but just to clear the trees so that those who follow you may enjoy the harvest?"

The discouraged missionary admitted that he had never thought of it in that way, and he didn't live long enough to see it turn out that way. But the old farmer was right, for other missionaries went to that field and it eventually provided a bountiful harvest for the Lord.

We may at times be tempted to become discouraged about the work of missionaries we support, but we need to remember that God's timetable for the harvest may be different from the timetable we are using. The apostle Paul recognized this fact when he wrote about his efforts at Corinth: "I have planted, Apollos watered; but God gave the increase" (1 Corinthians 3:6, KJV).

INDEX OF SCRIPTURES